¡Tu increíble cuerpo! / Your Amazing Body!

TU BOCA
YOUR MOUTH

Nancy Greenwood
Traducido por / Translated by Esther Ortiz

Gareth Stevens
PUBLISHING

Please visit our website, www.garethstevens.com. For a free color catalog of all our high-quality books, call toll free 1-800-542-2595 or fax 1-877-542-2596.

Library of Congress Cataloging-in-Publication Data

Names: Greenwood, Nancy, author.
Title: Your mouth = Tu boca / Nancy Greenwood.
Description: New York : Gareth Stevens Publishing, [2019] | Series: Your amazing body! = ¡Tu increíble cuerpo! | Includes index.
Identifiers: LCCN 2017046104| ISBN 9781538227404 (library bound)
Subjects: LCSH: Mouth–Juvenile literature.
Classification: LCC QM306 .G74 2019 | DDC 612.3/1–dc23
LC record available at https://lccn.loc.gov/2017046104

Published in 2019 by
Gareth Stevens Publishing
111 East 14th Street, Suite 349
New York, NY 10003

Translator: Esther Ortiz
Editorial Director, Spanish: Nathalie Beullens-Maoui
Editor, English: Kate Mikoley
Designer: Bethany Perl

Photo credits: Cover, p. 1 (boy) Dean Drobot/Shutterstock.com; p. 1 (playground) Stor24/Shutterstock.com; p. 5 AJP/Shutterstock.com; p. 7 didesign021/Shutterstock.com; p. 9 Daxiao Productions/Shutterstock.com; p. 11 LumineImages/Shutterstock.com; p. 13 wavebreakmedia/Shutterstock.com; p. 15 Yuliya Evstratenko/Shutterstock.com; p. 17 ERainbow/Shutterstock.com; p. 19 Tom Gowanlock/Shutterstock.com; p. 21 KK Tan/Shutterstock.com; p. 23 Littlekidmoment/Shuttestock.com.

Printed in the United States of America

CPSIA compliance information: Batch #CS18GS: For further information contact Gareth Stevens, New York, New York at 1-800-542-2595.

Contenido

Contents

Usas tu boca todo
el tiempo.

....

You use your mouth
all the time.

La usas para sonreir.

••••••••••••••••••••••••••••••

You use it to smile.

¡Te ayuda también
a hacer caras chistosas!

....

It helps you make
silly faces, too!

Usas tu boca
para hablar.

....

You use your mouth
to talk.

Hablamos bajito.
Se llama susurrar.

....

We talk quietly.
This is called whispering.

Usas la boca
para respirar.
También usas la nariz.

....

You use your mouth
to breathe.
You use your nose, too.

La boca tiene varias partes.
Los labios están afuera.

....

Mouths have many parts.
Lips are on the outside.

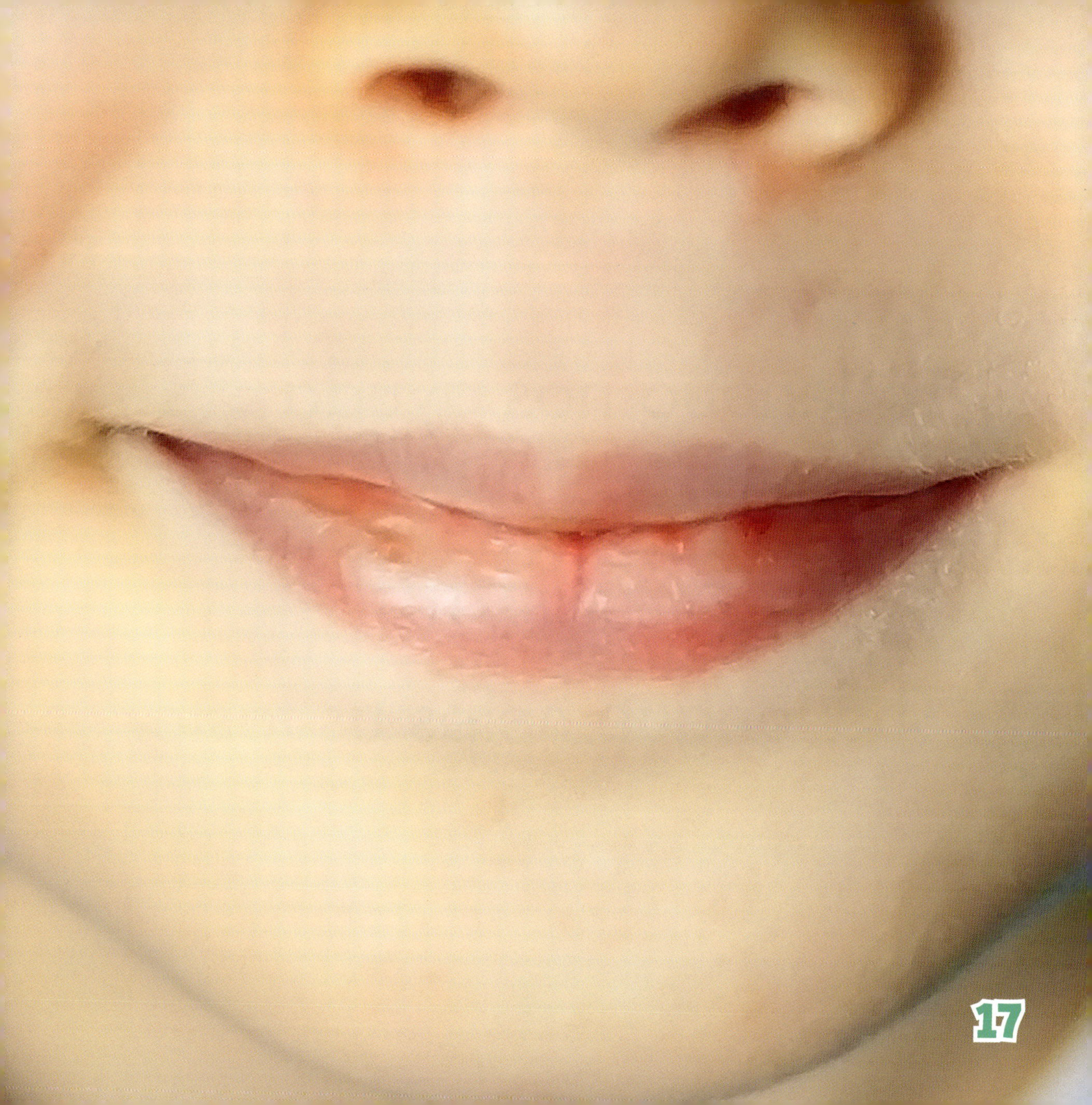

La lengua nos ayuda
a saborear.

....

The tongue helps us taste.

Los dientes están
en la boca.
Nos ayudan a masticar.

....

Teeth are in the mouth.
They help us chew.

Debemos limpiar nuestros dientes. Esto se llama cepillarse.

....

We need to clean our teeth. This is called brushing.

Palabras que debes aprender
Words to Know

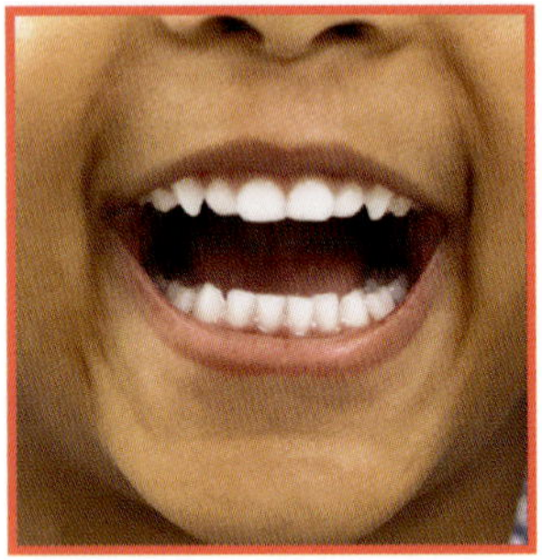

sonreir
smile

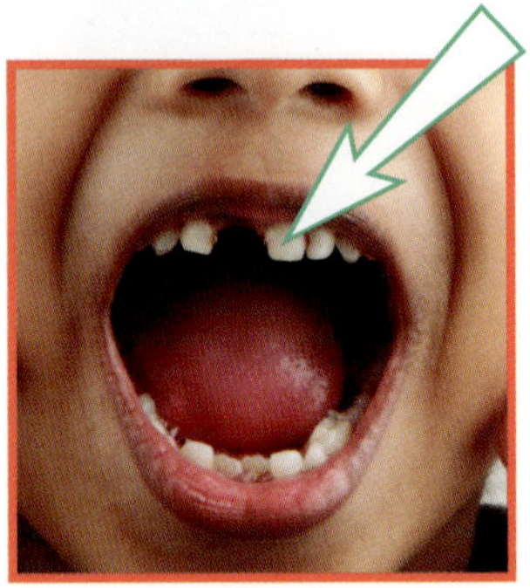

(los) dientes
teeth

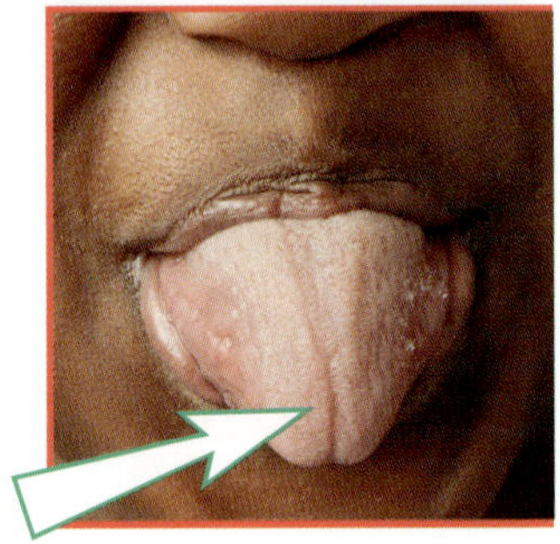

(la) lengua
tongue

Índice / Index